W9-ARG-913

Folding *for* Fun

origami for ages 4 and up

Didier Boursin

FIREFLY BOOKS

A FIREFLY BOOK

Published by Firefly Books Ltd. 2007

Copyright © 2007 Dessain and Tolra/Larousse

Original title: Pliages pour Jouer, Larousse, Paris

First printing

Publisher Cataloging-in-Publication Data (U.S.)

Boursin, Didier.
    Folding for fun: origami for ages 4 and up / Didier Boursin.
 [64] p. : col. ill., photos. ;   cm.
Summary: An illustrated book of paper-folding projects, from accordion books to noisemakers.
ISBN-13: 978-1-55407-253-8
ISBN-10: 1-55407-253-0
ISBN-13: 978-1-55407-252-1 (pbk.)
ISBN-10: 1-55407-252-2 (pbk.)
    1. Paperwork – Juvenile literature.   I. Title.
736.98 dc22   TT870.B677 2007

Library and Archives Canada Cataloguing in Publication

Boursin, Didier.
    Folding for fun: origami for ages 4 and up / Didier Boursin.
ISBN-13: 978-1-55407-253-8 (bound)
ISBN-13: 978-1-55407-252-1 (pbk.)
ISBN-10: 1-55407-253-0 (bound)
ISBN-10: 1-55407-252-2 (pbk.)
    1. Paper work—Juvenile literature.   I. Title.
TT870.B6815 2007   j736'.98
C2006-906834-8

Published in the United States by
Firefly Books (U.S.) Inc.
P.O. Box 1338, Ellicott Station
Buffalo, New York 14205

Published in Canada by
Firefly Books Ltd.
66 Leek Crescent
Richmond Hill, Ontario L4B 1H1

Design: Sonya V. Thursby / Opus House Incorporated
Drawings: Didier Boursin
Translation: Linda Hilpold
Origami consultation: John Reid

Printed in Singapore

Acknowledgments
Thanks to Alexandra, Lilas, Maya, Nina, Sofia and Thomas…for kindly offering their cute little faces for our book.
Thanks to the city of Paris, which graciously allowed us to take photographs in André Citroën Park.

You may send your personal stories and comments to:
www.origami-creation.com

Contents

Introduction

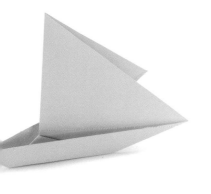

Using this book, you'll be able to make up your own games. In just a few minutes, you can fold a sheet of paper and create something you can play with right away.

The sailboat moves forward if you blow into its sails. The helicopter takes off spinning in the air. The firecracker explodes with a sharp crack. And the wobbly toy playfully runs down the staircase. Other fun origami projects await you and will amaze all your friends.

What will you need? A few simple sheets of paper, a pair of scissors and, especially, a good imagination.

Here are the symbols used in this book:

⟶▷ fold in front

⟶⊿ fold behind

► press with your finger

⟵✺ blow

↻▷ turn over

◯ hold at this point

⊥┈▷ slip the paper inside

Here are the main folds that you will use to make the origami projects in this book:

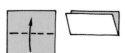 valley fold

  mountain fold

  mark the crease

  join the dots

everyday pleasures...

1, 2, 3 …

In your hands

A big-eared bunny

Here's a cute little bunny.
Look, its ears move when the bunny's happy!

You'll need
- a sheet of 8 1/2 x 11 inch (21.5 x 30 cm) paper
- a pair of scissors

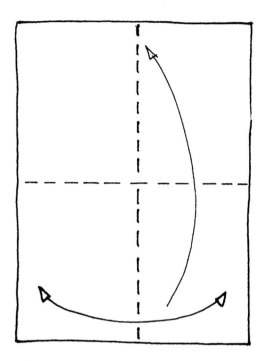

1 Fold the sheet of paper in half toward the top, then fold and unfold in half horizontally.

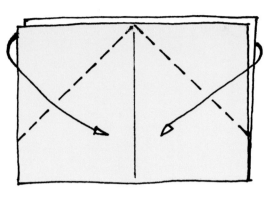

2 Fold over the sides to the center.

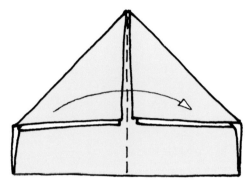

3 Fold in half.

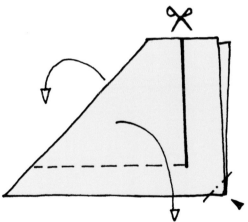

4 Cut along the thick line, then fold back the flap on each side. To make the nose, press in the tip.

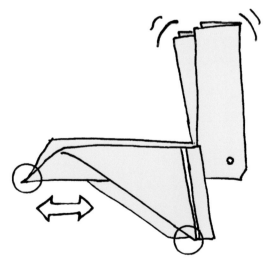

5 To make your bunny's ears move, hold at the points shown while pulling and pushing with your left hand.

Hello, my pet ...

Open your sheet of paper, then close it.
Your bird is hungry! If only it could talk!

You'll need
- a sheet of 8 1/2 × 11 inch (21.5 × 30 cm) paper
- a thick sheet of 8 1/2 × 11 inch colored paper
- a glue stick
- a pair of scissors

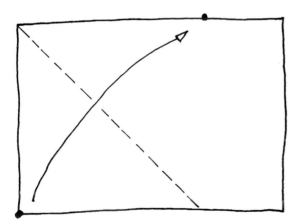

1 Fold the sheet of paper by joining the dots.

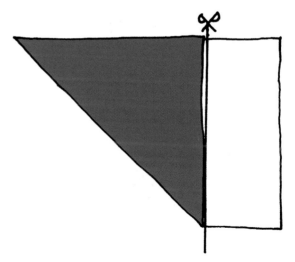

2 Cut the strip. You'll use this next.

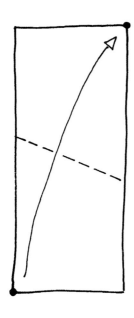

3 Fold the strip of paper in half by joining the dots.

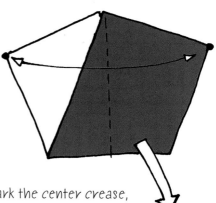

4 Mark the center crease, then unfold the paper completely.

5 Fold the paper across, along the fold.

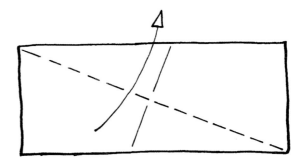

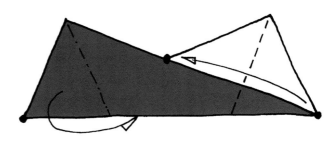

6 Fold both sides to the edge, as shown.

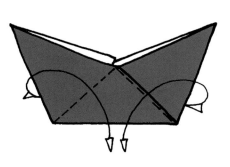

7 Crease the triangle at the center in both directions, then unfold the sides.

8 Fold the paper across, along the fold.

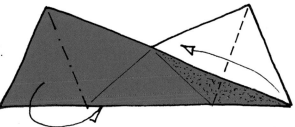

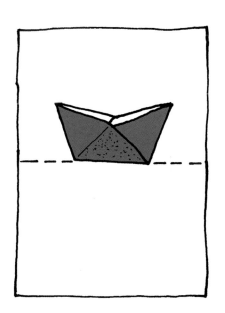

9 Fold the thicker sheet of paper in half, and place the origami on the center crease. Now glue the shaded area to both sides of the paper.

It balances ...

Oh, what a surprise! If you place this delicate mobile on your finger, it starts to turn all by itself. Watch it rock back and forth without ever losing its balance.

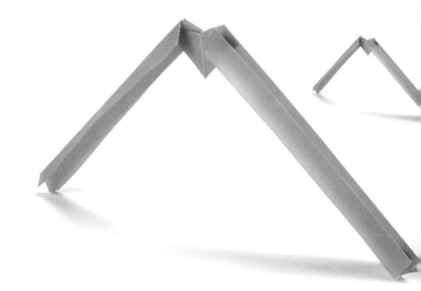

You'll need

- a sheet of 8 1/2 x 11 inch (21.5 x 30 cm) paper
- a pair of scissors

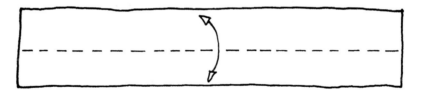

1 Cut a 1 1/2 inch (4.5 cm) strip lengthwise along the sheet. The strip should be 1 1/2 x 11 inches (4.5 x 30 cm). Mark the center crease and turn over.

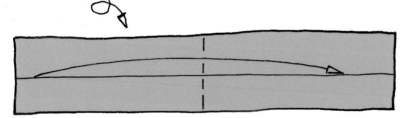

2 Fold in half toward the right.

3 Crease the upper corner fold, then fold over a flap, flattening the corner with your finger.

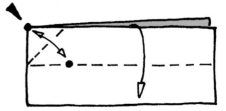

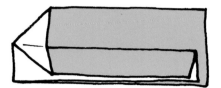

4 Like this, then turn over.

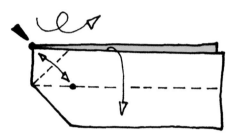

5 Repeat the same thing on the other side.

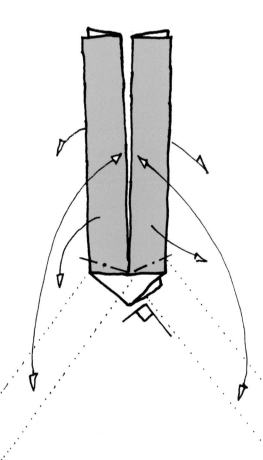

6 Fold down the legs as shown by the dotted line, then raise them.

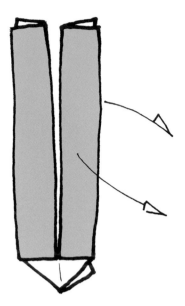

7 Pull one leg down by spreading apart the origami.

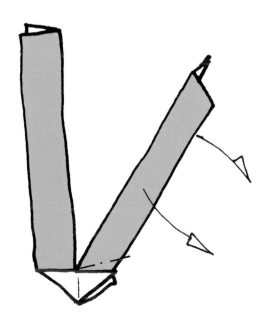

8 Continue the downward motion.

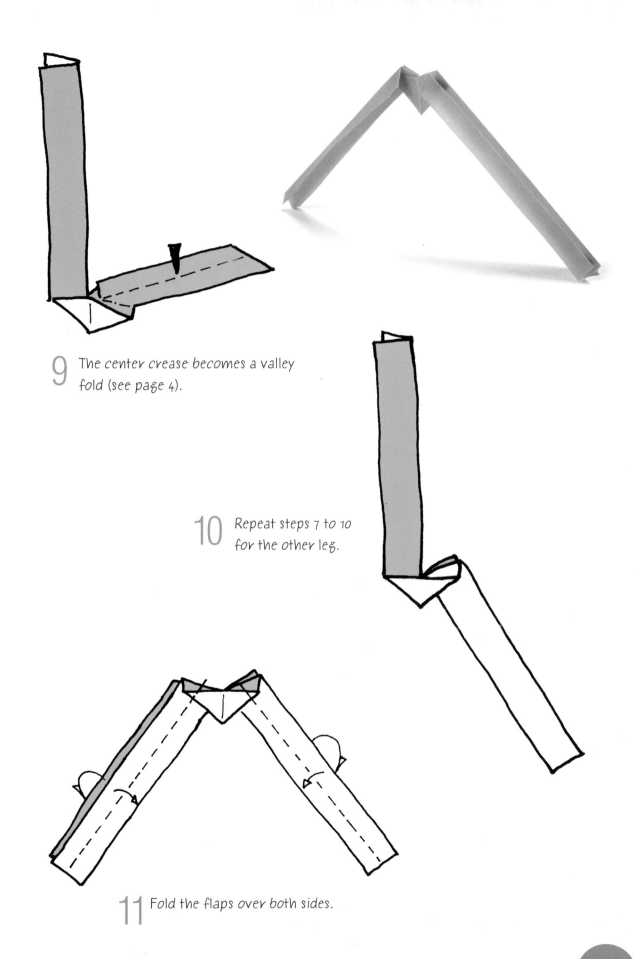

9 The center crease becomes a valley fold (see page 4).

10 Repeat steps 7 to 10 for the other leg.

11 Fold the flaps over both sides.

And yet, it spins!

Here's a magic trick that will surprise your friends. Place this propeller on your finger and it will begin to spin, making loops and crazy circles in the air.

You'll need
- colored tissue paper
- a pair of scissors

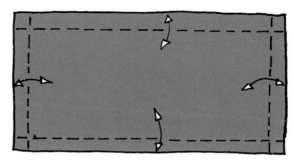

1 Take the tissue paper and cut out a 2 x 3 inch (5 x 7 cm) rectangle. Mark a regular crease to create a border, then turn over.

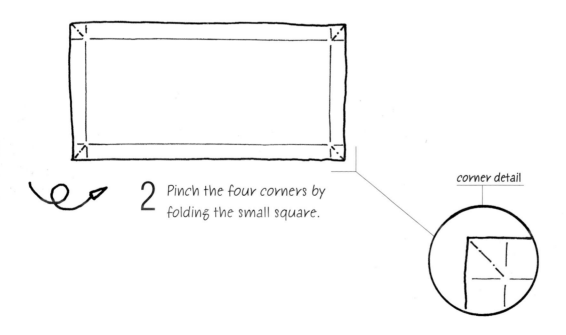

2 Pinch the four corners by folding the small square.

corner detail

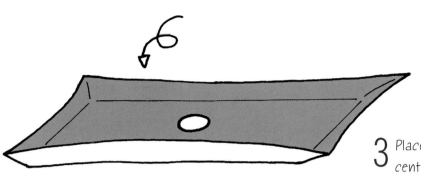

3 Place your thumb inside, in the center at the point shown, with your index finger on the outside. Move your hand forward, with the propeller in a vertical position, and remove your thumb. Your propeller will start to spin around your index finger as soon as you take away your thumb.

Magical designs

In your hands, the designs change like a kaleidoscope. One side, two sides...It's up to you to discover the third, hidden side — and the six designs.

You'll need
- a sheet of 8 1/2 x 11 inch (21.5 x 30 cm) paper
- a pair of scissors
- felt pens, colored pencils

1 Cut a 1 1/2 x 11 inch (4.5 x 30 cm) strip from the sheet of paper. Mark the middle of the strip.

2 Fold the upper triangle by joining the dots.

3 Fold back the strip along the triangle.

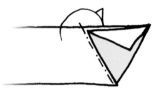

4 Repeat this fold right to the end.

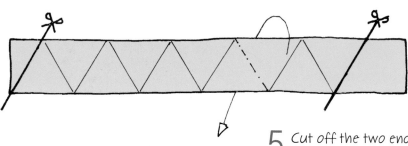

5 Cut off the two ends so that only ten triangles remain. Then fold behind the three triangles on the right.

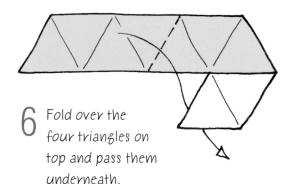

6 Fold over the four triangles on top and pass them underneath.

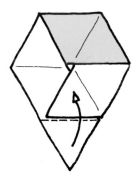

7 Glue the bottom triangle by folding it back over the other.

The steps to follow to discover different sides...

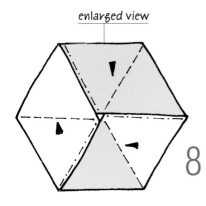

enlarged view

8 Draw a *colorful pattern* on both sides, then fold as shown.

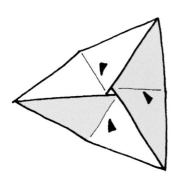

9 Join the three parts together.

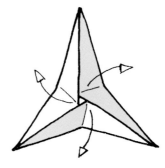

10 The *center* opens up and another blank side appears. Draw another *colorful pattern* by pressing backward in the middle. The fold turns over and returns to the position described in step 8.

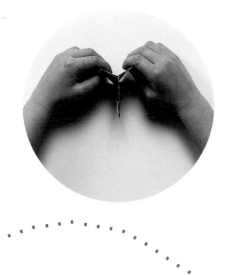

Adventure diary

You're the writer. Will you write a funny story? Create a comic strip? Send a fancy invitation to celebrate your birthday? It's up to you to write all your secrets.

You'll need
- a sheet of 8 1/2 x 11 inch (21.5 x 30 cm) paper
- a pair of scissors
- felt pens, colored pencils

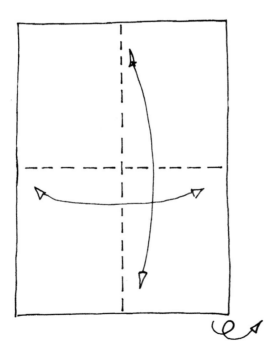

1 Mark the middle of the sheet of paper by folding it in both directions, then turn it over.

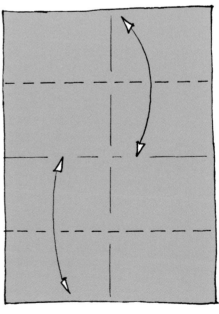

2 Crease the upper middle and the lower middle.

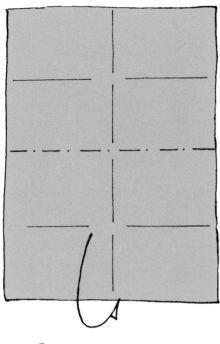

3 Fold in half behind.

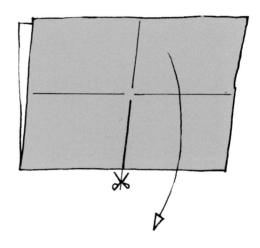

4 Cut along the thick line. Then unfold the upper part and turn the paper horizontally.

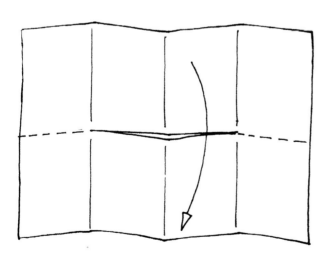

5 Fold over the upper part.

Tibili's story

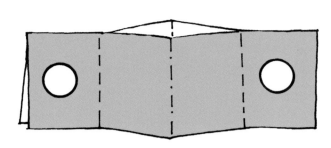

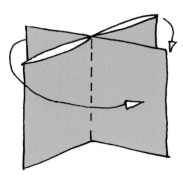

6 Bring the sides together by holding the ends.

7 Gather together all the pages.

Tip
You can also fold a bigger sheet of paper to make a bigger notebook.
Take a sheet of 17 x 24 inch (43 x 61 cm) paper, or use colorful folders.

Once you have finished your book, you can easily make several copies. All you need to do is unfold it and make a color photocopy. You can also draw in black only, photocopy the pages, and then color them.

Pop, pop, pop

Here's an origami project that will make noise during recess. It makes a sound as loud as a firecracker! Now it's your turn to play.

You'll need
- a sheet of 8 1/2 × 11 inch (21.5 × 30 cm) paper
- a pair of scissors

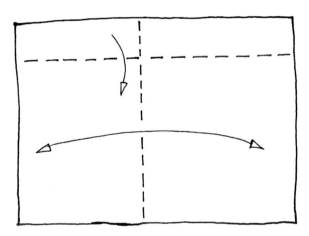

1 Mark the center crease of a sheet of 8 1/2 × 11 inch (21.5 × 30 cm) paper, then fold a strip.

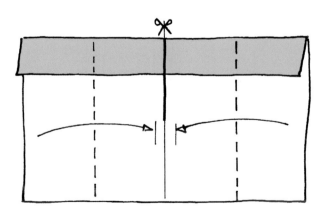

2 Fold over the sides, leaving a space in the center. Then cut along the thick line.

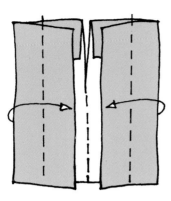

3 Fold over the flaps,
then join the sides.

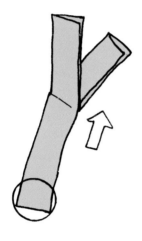

4 Place your fingers on
both sides of the fold
to create a V. By
quickly sliding your
fingers to the top,
the two ends snap
against each other.

Moo! Moo!

The little flap at the end of the straw vibrates, imitating the sound of a cow or a lamb.

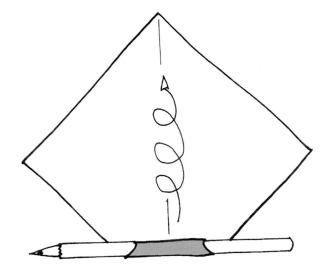

1 Take a square sheet of paper, or cut out a square from a sheet of paper. Tightly roll the square paper around a pencil. Gently remove the pencil.

2 Glue the straw, then pinch one end.

enlarged view

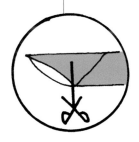

3 Using scissors, snip one of the ends. Be careful not to cut it off.

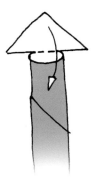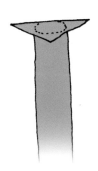

4 Fold back the little flap onto the straw.

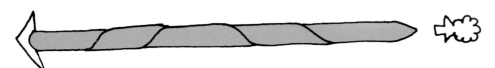

5 Blow gently to make a sound. You can have fun making different kinds of whistles that will produce a different sound each time. The narrower the whistle, the higher the sound.

4,5,6 … Let me go

let me fly . . .

Ready for takeoff

Your attention please. Prepare for takeoff. The last passengers heading for Mars are asked to go to the boarding gate.

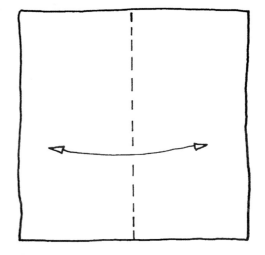

1 Use a square sheet of paper, or cut a square out of a sheet of 8 1/2 × 11 inch (21.5 × 30 cm) paper. Mark the center crease.

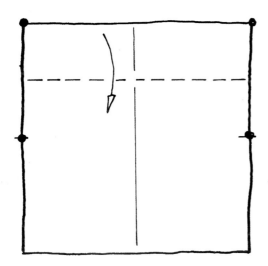

2 Fold the top down to the middle.

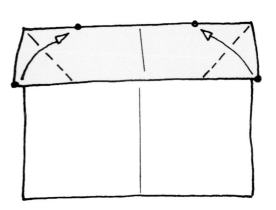

3 Fold the corners by joining the dots.

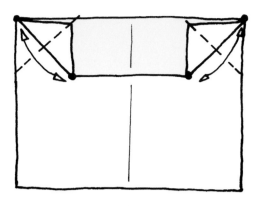

4 Fold and unfold the corners.

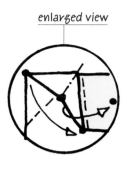

5 Flatten them by joining the dots.

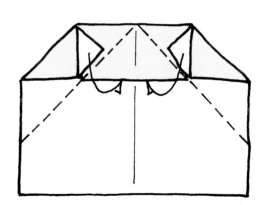

6 Fold the sides along the center crease, sliding the triangle underneath.

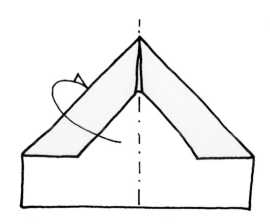

7 Fold the paper in half behind.

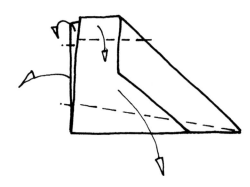

8 Fold the upper edges, then fold the paper as shown.

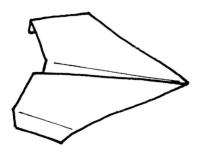

9 Before launching, raise the wings. Your airplane should be able to fly very far and for a long time. You and your friends can organize a competition based on the longest time or distance traveled.

Who's going to win the boat race?
The one who makes it to port without
sinking.

You'll need
- a sheet of 8 1/2 x 11 inch
  (21.5 x 30 cm) paper

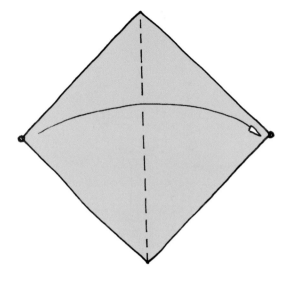

1 Take a small square piece of paper,
or cut out a square from a sheet of
8 1/2 x 11 inch (21.5 x 30 cm) paper.
Fold in half as shown.

2 Fold to the horizontal.

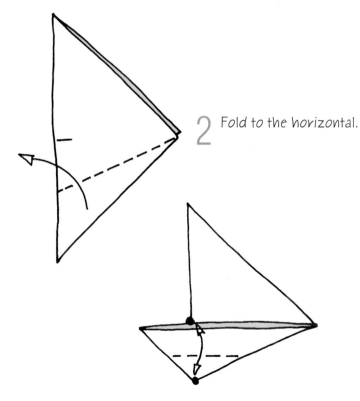

3 Fold by joining the dots,
then unfold completely.

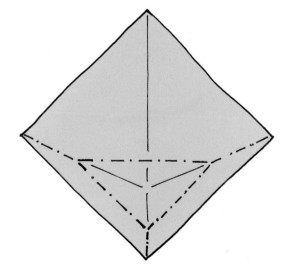

4 Crease the triangle and the sides well,
using a mountain fold (see page 4).

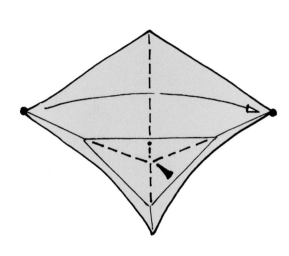

5 Create a hollow in the center while folding the paper in half.

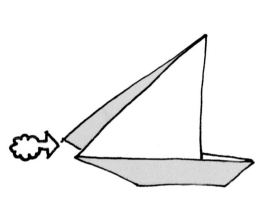

6 Blow into the sails to make the sailboat move forward.

Here's a little boat that floats on the water.

You'll need

- a sheet of 8 1/2 × 11 inch (21.5 × 30 cm) paper
- a pair of scissors

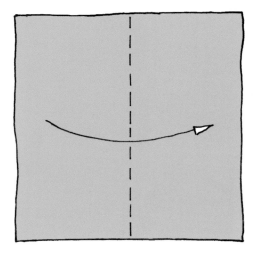

1 Create a large 8 1/2 × 8 1/2 inch (21.5 × 21.5 cm) square from the sheet of paper. Crease the center line of the square.

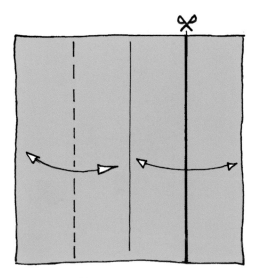

2 Crease each side, then cut away one strip of paper.

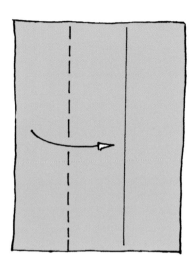

3 Fold the strip on the left.

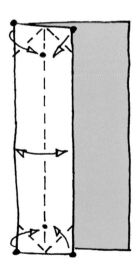

4 Crease the middle of this strip, then fold the four corners as shown.

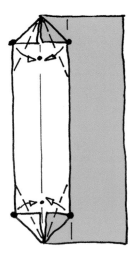

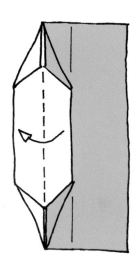

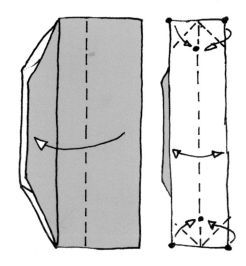

5 Fold over the ends.

6 Fold the right flap over the other.

7 Now, fold the strip on the right. Then repeat steps 4 to 7.

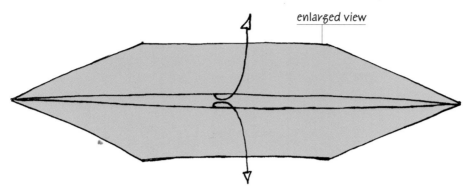

enlarged view

8 Open up the boat by pulling apart the sides.

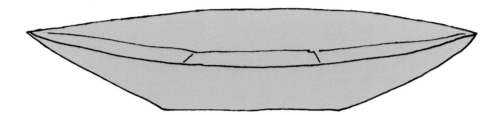

Prepare to sail off!

Blowing in the wind

This funny helicopter spins when you drop it. You can also pull it behind you on a string.

You'll need
- a sheet of 8 1/2 × 11 inch (21.5 × 30 cm) paper
- a pair of scissors
- a needle and some thread

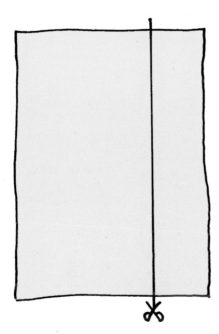

1 Cut a 2 inch (6 cm) wide strip along the length of the sheet of paper to create a 2 × 11 inch (6 × 30 cm) rectangle.

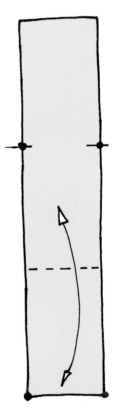

2 Crease one fold by folding over one-third of the strip.

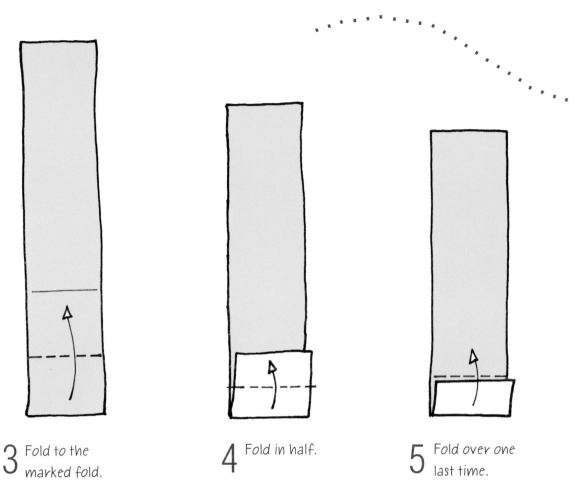

3 Fold to the
marked fold.

4 Fold in half.

5 Fold over one
last time.

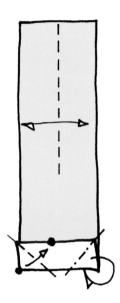

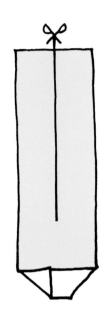

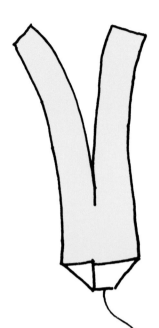

6 Fold the corners, one in front and the other behind. Mark the center crease.

7 Using your scissors, cut as shown.

8 Using a needle, place a thread in the middle of the tip. Then curve the blades of your helicopter very slightly, in opposite directions.

Pirouettes

Climb a tree or to the top of the stairs and let your origami go. Like magic, it spins around, performing pirouettes.

You'll need
- a small square sheet of paper

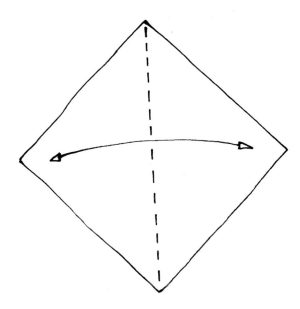

1 Take a small piece of square paper about 3 1/2 × 3 1/2 inches (9 × 9 cm), or cut out a square from a sheet of 8 1/2 × 11 inch (21.5 × 30 cm) paper. Crease the vertical fold.

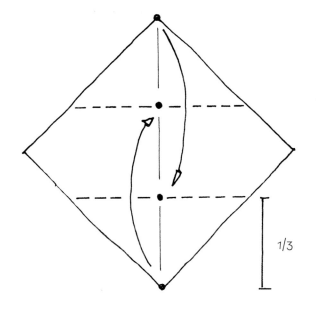

1/3

2 Fold in thirds along the center crease.

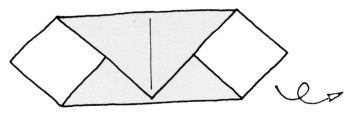

3 It should look like this.
Turn over the paper.

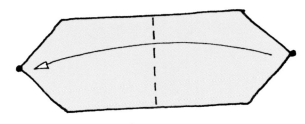

4 Fold in half.

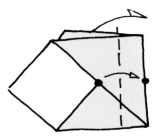

5 Fold back the
two sides by
joining the dots,
then flatten the
paper.

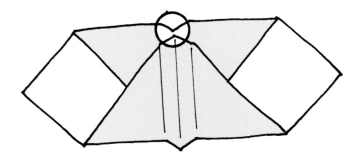

6 Hold your origami at
the point shown, then
let it go. Watch how
it quickly spins!

What a ball

One ball, two balls, three balls. You juggle with ease, and suddenly all your friends are watching you.

You'll need
- a small square sheet of paper

1 Take a square sheet of paper, or cut out a square from a sheet of 8 1/2 × 11 inch (21.5 × 30 cm) paper. Mark the horizontal crease.

2 Mark the vertical crease.

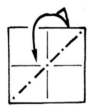

3 Mark the first diagonal by making a mountain fold (see page 4).

4 Mark the second one the same way.

5 It should look like this.

6 Hold your square in both hands. Create a hollow, then flatten.

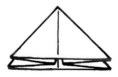

7 You should have a triangle.

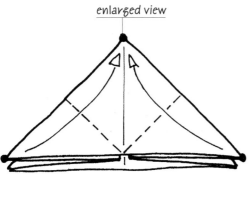

enlarged view

8 Raise the sides.

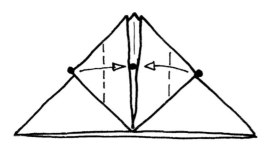

9 Fold the flaps toward the center.

10 Fold down the upper tips.

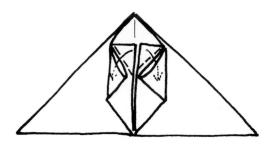

11 Slide the triangles into the pockets on the sides...

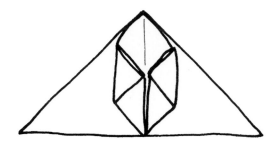

12 ...like this, then turn over the paper.

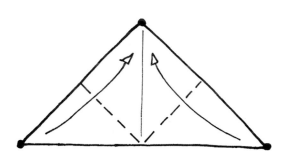

13 Repeat steps 8 to 12 on the other side.

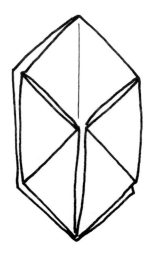

14 To inflate your ball, quickly blow into the bottom.

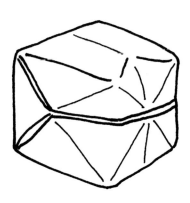

15 Check that the ball is fully blown up before starting to play.

And—oopsy daisy—

Your origami toy does somersaults. You can line up a series of toys. Have fun making them fall in single file down the stairs.

You'll need
- a small square sheet of paper

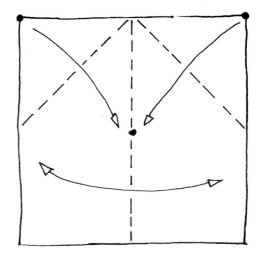

1. Take a small 6 × 6 inch (15 × 15 cm) square of paper, or cut out a square from a sheet of 8 1/2 × 11 inch (21.5 × 30 cm) paper. Mark the center crease, then fold the sides by joining the dots.

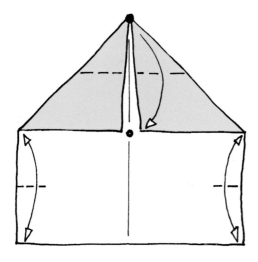

2. Fold the tip in half and mark the middle on the lower part.

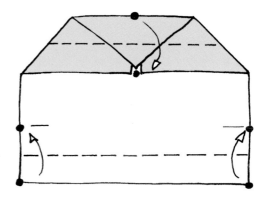

3. Fold the upper part in half. Then fold the bottom by joining the dots.

a somersault!

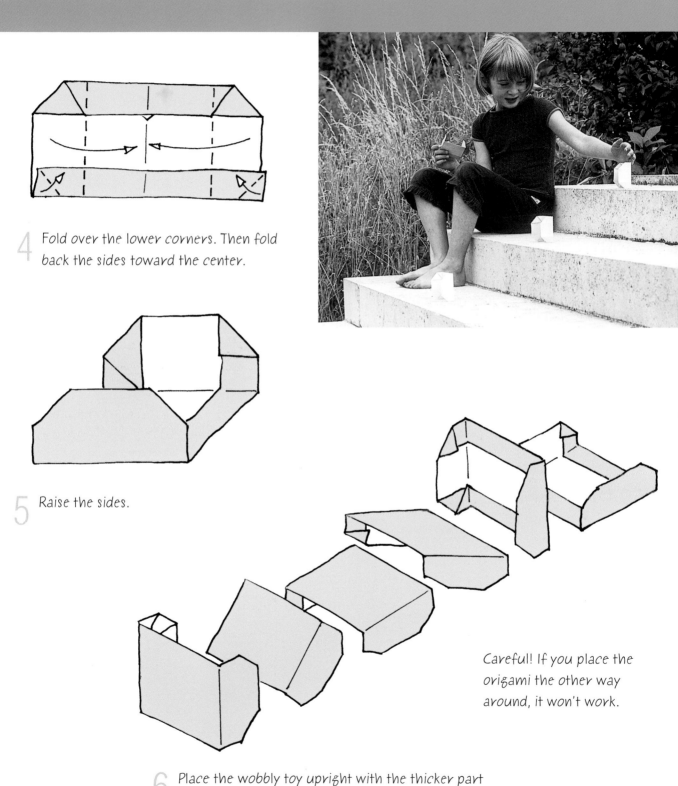

4 Fold over the lower corners. Then fold back the sides toward the center.

5 Raise the sides.

Careful! If you place the origami the other way around, it won't work.

6 Place the wobbly toy upright with the thicker part at the top. Then gently push it so it moves.

This is the story of a poor fisherman who sets out one morning in his little boat to fish. Returning to port, he opens his nets and discovers a magic fish. Now it's your turn to tell your own tale by folding and unfolding your envelope.

You'll need

- a 4 1/8 × 9 1/2 inch (10.5 × 24 cm) envelope
- a pair of scissors

Heading off to fish

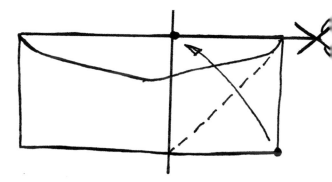

1 Seal the envelope by gluing the flap. Cut open the top of the envelope. Fold the right edge to the top edge by joining the dots.

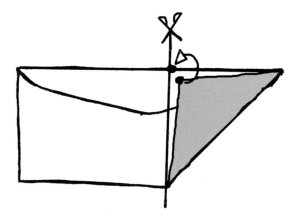

2 Using your scissors, cut downward, as shown, so that you have a square when you open the fold. Be careful not to cut through all the layers of the envelope. Your square should be sealed on two sides.

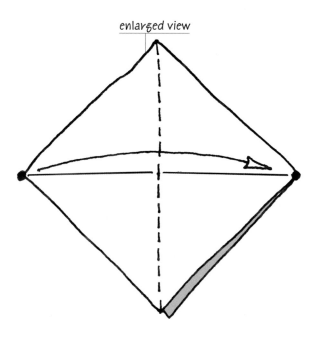

enlarged view

3 Unfold the square with the open side down. Mark the center crease.

boat turns into a fish

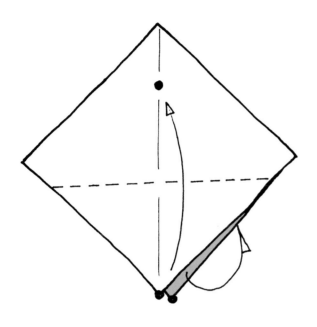

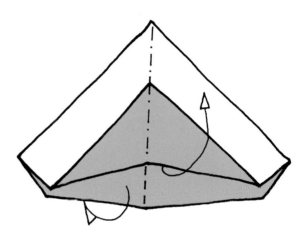

4 Raise the tips of each side by joining the dots.

5 Spread open the sides, then flatten the paper.

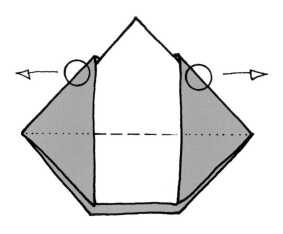

6 Pull the sides by holding them at the points shown.

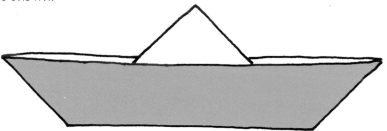

7 Here's the fisherman's boat!

Caught in the net...

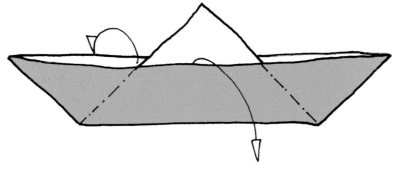

8 Spread apart the sides by flattening them.

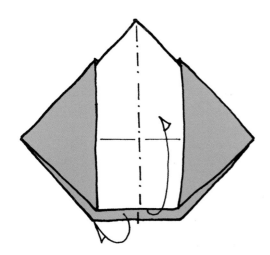

9 Spread open the sides, then flatten them.

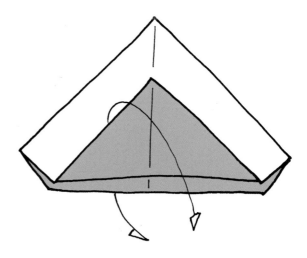

10 Unfold the triangles.

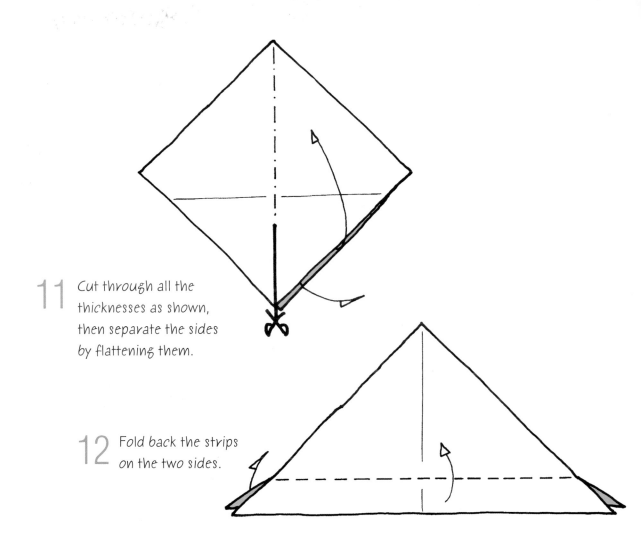

11 Cut through all the thicknesses as shown, then separate the sides by flattening them.

12 Fold back the strips on the two sides.

Here's the fisherman's hat!

13 Open the sides once again.

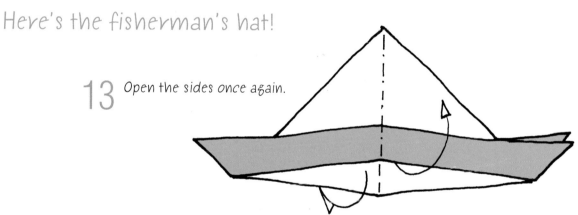

14 Fold the triangles onto the two sides... to make a fish appear. Magic!

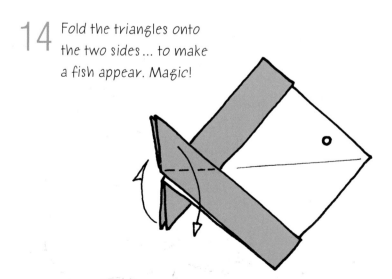